Weddir

Planning

Guide

Guide to Checklists, Tricks and Ideas For Planning and
Organizing Every Aspect of Your Dream Wedding While
Also Saving a Lot of Money and Nerves

By Lisa Grisham

Contents

Thank you for buying this book and I hope that you will find it useful. If you will want to share your thoughts on this book, you can do so by leaving a review on the Amazon page, it helps me out a lot.

Introduction

When it pertains to wedding planning, it's challenging to get rid of a few of the aspects that are most significant to you. With this guide to planning the best wedding on a budget plan, you won't need to.

In This book You Are Going To Find Out:

- How To Lessen Expenses Without Compromising
- How to Spare Cash On All Of Your Wedding Expenses
- How To Recognize Vendors who Are Over-Charging
- How To Plan Your Wedding From Top to Bottom
- Planning The Most Unforgettable Wedding Day Feasible.

Chapter 1: How to Plan a Wedding On A Budget plan.

Congratulations on your upcoming wedding! Planning a wedding ought to be the most unforgettable experience of your life. Besides, you will start a brand-new adventure shared with the person you love.

Sadly, when it pertains to wedding planning, unless you have an endless budget plan, it could be an aggravating and overwhelming undertaking. Initially, you need to establish your budget plan, and after that, you want to do your finest to remain inside this amount, which typically indicates cutting corners and getting rid of a few of the essential features and aspects of your day.

Weddings are exceptionally costly if you take the conventional path without knowing how to negotiate expenses or handle suppliers.

With this book, nevertheless, you are getting approaches for sparing cash on all facets of your wedding planning in addition to making sure that your day goes perfectly.

You are worthy of the best wedding, and with money-saving ideas and methods, I really believe that you are going to have the ability to accomplish this.

Step One: Figure out Your Budget

To start, you want to take a seat with your partner and identify a sensible budget plan. Examine your financial resources and just how much you are both comfy with spending.

This isn't the time to figure out the expenses of each aspect; it's simply taking the initial step in your wedding planning and choosing, together, what your wedding fund is going to be. The Pre-Planning Stage is a vital step in making sure that you are on track and arranged.

Numerous couples neglect this really essential part and begin planning their wedding without a firm budget plan in mind. This is going to make things extremely challenging when you find yourself out of time and cash, without the wedding planned and all set for your special day.

Take a seat together and figure out a reasonable budget plan. You can constantly change the budget plan later down the road if required, but for now, be open with one another, go over possible numbers up until you come to a sensible budget plan without leaving you both having a hard time paying off a huge financial obligation when you start your married life.

After all, your wedding is a festivity of your love, and the last thing you wish to do is to enter into a marriage where you are attached to a debt that is going to take years to settle. Consider what your goals are for the initial year of your marital relationship.

Do you wish to put a down payment on a home? Take a prolonged trip? You are going to want to completely analyze what your budget plan is going to be while enabling you both the capability to save for your future long after the wedding is over.

It's simple to get delighted about your wedding planning and get big loans or borrow from family and friends without thinking about how challenging it might be to pay it back gradually.

Consider your family and friends who might have an interest in aiding with specific elements of your wedding. Possibly you have a cousin who is a floral designer or an auntie who would be more than pleased to play the piano throughout your event.

You'd be amazed at simply how many expensive aspects you can remove by taking family and friends into consideration for certain activities. Most importantly, they are going to be delighted that you are including them in your big day!

When thinking about your budget plan, remember that most of a wedding budget plan is generally for the reception. The food, beverages, rentals, and location that you select are going to use up a big part of your budget plan, based upon the kind of food offered, the number of attendees and whether you are footing the whole bill or having family and friends bake, cook and assist.

Your wedding apparel is going to use up an approximated 20% of your budget plan too, and your videographer and photographer another 10-20%. You might decide to have a buddy video the wedding event for you, in addition to a buddy or member of the family that you trust, taking your photos. This is going to spare a great deal of cash on your wedding. Nevertheless, be cautious with who you pick as you are never going to have the ability to record your wedding event once again.

If you discover that your budget plan is far too little, begin sparing weekly by choosing to place a particular amount away. You might open a bank account which is utilized solely for your wedding event.

Step 2: Pre-Planning

In order to start preparing for your wedding event, you are going to both want to discuss what the most crucial elements and features of your day are going to be. Based upon lifestyles or religious beliefs, you both might have particular aspects that you feel need to be featured, and these can impact the budget plan, so it is vital that you jot down the "no bargain" elements of your wedding which you simply can not be without.

If you haven't yet picked a date, this is the time to work on doing so. Consider in which season you ought to have your wedding event (thinking about the attendees and their vacation time or capability to participate due to work), along with whether you are aiming to have a wedding in your area or away.

The most costly months in which to get wed are spring, summer season, and early fall, along with the Christmas and Valentine's Day holidays. In case you have a wedding that happens in the late fall or early winter season, you are going to have the ability to reduce expenses considerably.

Additionally, think about the day of the week, as this is going to have an effect on your location expenses additionally. Weddings that happen throughout a weekday are normally much more economical than a weekend wedding, where locations are in demand, and more couples are attempting to book locations. Many times, suppliers are going to negotiate on expenses in case you book throughout an "off day" due to the fact that they understand they are less probable to fill that area otherwise.

And lastly, the time of day additionally plays a part in expenses. Normally, weddings which happen sooner in the day are going to cost less than early evening, late afternoon wedding occasions.

Attempt to be versatile with the date you pick, specifically in case it is going to assist you to extend the budget plan even further, allowing you to spare cash or spend it on other components of your big day which you may otherwise not have the ability to pay for.

Here are a couple of other questions you are going to want to go over prior to going past the pre-planning stage:

- How many attendees would you like to have? Jot down all of the buddies and family that you want to see the most. (Generate your "must attend" list initially).
- What kind of location would you want to be wed in? Would you like a luxurious indoor reception, a tinier informal reception, outside garden reception?
- What element of your big day is essential to you both?
- Are you going to have a band or a DJ at your reception? DJs are generally much more budget-friendly than a band.
- How many bridesmaids, groomsmen, and other party members do you want to have?
- Should your wedding have a particular motif, and if yes, what would it be?
- Are you going to have an open bar, minimal or none whatsoever?
- Are you going to have a sit-down supper or a buffet-style reception?
- Where would wish to spend your honeymoon?

These are simply a couple of the numerous questions that you are going to want to go over, and while the budget plan is going to be impacted depending upon your selections, you can constantly trim down if that's what you decide.

Book off a weekend when your partner and you are able to discuss your wedding, far from disturbance and noise. Jot down suggestions, notes, and ideas that you both have for your wedding and what you think are the most crucial aspects.

This is really essential if you wish to understand each other and make sure that you feature the elements that are going to make your day additionally special.

Keep in mind, these are basic questions concerning your wedding preparation that are going to provide you with an excellent idea regarding what your partner and you imagine as the „ best wedding. " Absolutely nothing is written in stone, and as you start to prepare for your big day, you are probably going to wind up altering particular components, reducing a few of the unneeded expenses and designing your big day so that it incorporates all of the crucial aspects while removing the expensive components which aren't as essential.

I have actually seen many couples shocked at simply how many suggestions their partner has for their big day. Ladies, don't disregard your partner, and it's very probable he has suggestions on what he wants to see just like you do.

It's crucial that you maintain an open mind and listen to one another. Does one desire an extravagant reception while the other favors a straightforward buffet-style banquet?

Do your finest to talk now prior to planning your special day so that there are hardly any dissatisfactions or surprises in the future. Work out any compromises and differences where required. Besides, this is an extremely big day for both of you, and you ought to both have a huge part in the preparation.

Step 3: Get Organized

The most budget-friendly weddings are ones which are well arranged, well prepared, and well planned. If you begin your wedding planning without jotting down all the things that you require, you might ignore a crucial aspect that you are going to require to squeeze into your budget plan in the future, so it's crucial to keep an in-depth list of all the things that have to get arranged.

In case you have Microsoft Excel, you are going to discover that it is incredibly simple to produce duty lists along with keeping precise records of all the things from contacts, suppliers to your attendee list (including their contact number, addresses, who has actually replied to your invites, etc.). You can additionally utilize Excel to keep an up-to-date list of presents from your wedding to ensure that you are able to send thank you notes in the future.

In case you are not tech-savvy, you could buy a wedding organizer, which is a straightforward note pad which contains pockets and envelopes for essential memos and notes. You could discover these at your neighborhood stationery store, or you can merely produce one with a paper, binder, separators and tabs.

Whenever you speak with a supplier that you have an interest in dealing with, request a business card to ensure that you are able to include it to your organizer for follow up. Make certain that you have contact information and contact number for everybody associated with the preparation of your wedding, consisting of floral designers, DJs, reception sites, photographers and catering services.

This organizer is going to additionally be a terrific memory book in the future, long after your wedding is done! You might additionally include your wedding photos and CDs to it, producing a scrapbook memento.

When I made my wedding organizer, I added in a "Journal," which enabled me to reflect back in the future, and share my feelings and thoughts with my loved ones and buddies. Later, when I had my child, I planned on handing it over to her to ensure that she might comprehend how each bride-to-be goes through the nerves, the aggravation, and the secret worries when organizing the wedding.

Refer to your organizer often and keep up to date on the progress you have actually made. In case you are preparing your wedding completely by yourself without the aid of a wedding organizer, you are going to discover your wedding planning note pad and your journal to be an extraordinary resource in guaranteeing that you have covered all bases and that you have a contact list accessible when you require it.

As your big day draw near, you are going to wish to produce what is called a "timeline of events." This is going to consist of all of the important things which you want to have performed, in order, before your special day.

Make certain to confirm with hired help and suppliers the time frame of every aspect of your wedding event (consisting of reception transitioning into a dance if you select to have one), and go over the service requirements with every supplier to ensure that you both comprehend what is anticipated.

Things To Keep In Mind

Talk with your photographer and videographer about the time of day which is ideal for your pictures along with other details that have to do with recording the whole event. Be REALLY particular in describing every element that you want recorded to stay clear of miscommunication or dissatisfaction in the future. Print a copy of your demands and hand that to each individual before your big day.

Discuss with your band or DJ about how long you want them to be there, consisting of any particular music or tracks you want to hear and in which order.

Print off a music sheet consisting of all of your demands and offer it to your band or DJ at least 2 weeks before your wedding event to make certain that they have the ability to play this music. You are also giving them time to ask any questions they might have beforehand.

Speak with your food caterer to have a grasp of how long cocktail hour is going to be in addition to discussing the starting and ending time of the dinner.

Speak to those transporting you to your reception and wedding to make sure that they know when to anticipate arrival and departure times. You also want to find out if there are several wedding celebrations being transported in an identical vehicle at various times.

Make certain you offer yourself a lot of time in the event of an unanticipated hold-up and bear in mind that receptions and weddings typically take longer than anticipated.

When producing your wedding event timeline, constantly include additional time just in case. There are numerous things that can take place all of a sudden, and by assigning a bit of additional time to each part, you are going to have the ability to keep your schedule constantly.

Chapter 2: Location

So, you've identified the month of your wedding event, and ideally, a handful of prospective dates. The next action is checking places and seeing what is out there in addition to the expenses.

The primary step is to choose whether you plan on having the wedding and reception at the identical place, and in case you do, it is going to cost far less. Nevertheless, depending upon the wedding size and the available locations, this may not be possible.

In case you do not have a specific wedding event venue or church in mind, think about leasing a hall for both your reception and wedding to spare cash. Open the phonebook and document the local places that are readily available, calling each one initially to identify expenses and availability. Hosting your reception and wedding at the identical location additionally spares money and time by having the ability to get rid of transport expenses.

Numerous couples additionally decide to hold their wedding events outdoors in gardens, local parks or beaches. This could lower expenses substantially. Nevertheless, it's really crucial to call your local city center to identify any limitations which might be in place, along with any associated expenses or costs.

Numerous couples decide to host their weddings at the houses of family members, in outside vineyards, gazebos and even where the bride and groom initially met. So long as your venue is a location which both of you feel linked to and is perfect for both of you, along with the wedding celebration (size being an aspect), go all out! It's irrelevant where you have your wedding as long as you are both delighted with your choice, and you can guarantee that it is able to accommodate your wedding attendees.

In case your ceremony venue is too little to feature your whole attendee list, you could additionally go with a personal wedding with a lesser number of attendees present, and open your reception site to your whole attendee list, to ensure that they can celebrate your wedding event with you while enabling your partner and you to have your real wedding event at a site which both of you are delighted with.

When it concerns your reception, bear in mind that specific suppliers are going to charge you for "unused space." This suggests that in case your attendee list is 100 and just 50 appear, you still might be required to pay for unused 50 seats. For that reason, it is essential to have a carefully approximated amount of attendees and to go over that with your supplier before scheduling the reception site to see whether you are going to be charged for anybody not coming to your wedding without previous notice.

The wedding place is typically discussed greatly in between couples, and often their family. Typically, the couple is going to wish to have their wedding in a non-traditional area while the family of one or both insists that it happens in a church.

It's a Hard Choice

On the one hand, you wish to make your moms and dads delighted. However, it's your wedding event. Eventually, you have to decide where to have the wedding. A wedding held by a waterfall or on the beach is no less legitimate than a wedding located in a synagogue or church.

In case you wish to have an Elvis-inspired wedding event in Sin city or a Star Trek-themed wedding on a mock Enterprise bridge, that's your decision! And your wedding event is still going to be just as legitimate as it would have been in case it was held right before the pearly gates!

There are a number of primary factors to consider when picking a wedding place. Initially, you ought to pick an area that your family and friends are going to have the ability to reach. In case you reside in Florida, asking your family and friends to all fly to Vegas with you might be out of the question. In case you want to have a tinier wedding with less of your family members, that's your decision. However, it's a thing to have in mind.

Next, it ought to be reasonably near to the place of the reception. In case you are holding your wedding on the beach, you may wish to hold the reception there, too. You may lease a great place close to the beach, or have the reception at a close-by hotel. However, asking attendees to drive 8 miles for the reception won't make anybody extremely pleased.

A wedding is a long, tiring occasion. After the wedding, individuals are going to be starving and tired, most likely. They want to be taken into a relaxing, calming environment rapidly and fed! So keep in mind to find the reception and wedding close together.

A fantastic idea for lots of couples is to have the wedding at the house of a relative or buddy. This produces a homier wedding event, and the reception could be held right on the grounds. This is definitely simpler logistically, however, it can additionally be extremely romantic to have a wedding event at the home where the bride-to-be grew up or the home where the groom's grandparents stated their vows!

Wherever you select, simply make certain it fits you both. This is a day you are always going to remember, and it ought to be in a location that is going to make both of you pleased. Don't fret about what anybody else claims. Pick the location that is going to make YOU the most happy.

Chapter 3: Saving Cash on Wedding Attire

As a bride-to-be, you are very likely currently imagining the ideal wedding gown. Whether you have an interest in a conventional, traditional, or modern style, it's best to start your search early on, months prior to your actual big day.

To start, scour the Web for wholesale discount bridal stores and wedding publications to figure out the style you have an interest in and to get an idea of the price range of every design. As you most likely understand, every site, each offline shop and every publication are going to have distinct prices, often for the identical gown, so it is essential to look around beforehand, so you aren't hurried into buying, days prior to your wedding event.

Considering that it's very probable that your dress might require modifications, it's yet another reason why you ought to buy your dress way ahead of time. Keep in mind to take into consideration your body size, type and the part of year you are getting wed. In case your wedding will be in the fall or winter season, long sleeves make good sense, or in case you are having a summer season wedding, something with brief sleeves would be more in fashion.

As soon as you have actually figured out the style and kind of bridal gown that you have an interest in, begin price shopping. Start with looking for local bridal stores in your location, along with looking on the web. The majority of online bridal stores provide a money-back guarantee to ensure that in case you are not pleased with the dress you got, you are going to have the ability to return it (unchanged) for a fast refund, however, make certain to go through the return policy and terms of service before purchasing.

You are going to additionally wish to make certain that in case you do buy a dress online, that the supplier offers Fed Ex or overnight shipping to ensure that you may quickly track where your shipment is. The final thing you desire is your dress being lost in transit, and that's why you want to demand that a tracking number is offered upon purchase.

In case you are acquiring your gown from a local bridal store, inquire about the price of working with an in-house seamstress, as it is frequently even more budget-friendly to work with an external seamstress for your changes.

If acquiring a dress isn't that significant to you, you might decide to lease your dress as well as the bridesmaid dresses and tuxedos for your wedding celebration. Go to your department stores for tuxedo leasings and ask as to whether there are any special deals, like the groom getting his tux rental free of charge in case the groomsmen rent their tuxedos there. Tux rentals typically consist of cufflinks, tie, vest, and often shoes, so don't forget to ask.

Otherwise, explore neighborhood outlets or thrift shops for pre-owned suits or tuxedos that are going to spare you a fortune while making sure your groom and his guys look wonderful!

Have the budget plan in mind when choosing gowns for your bridesmaids too. While a bridesmaid is typically going to buy her own gown, remember that weddings could be pricey for bridesmaids and search for affordable options for them. Numerous web shops offer affordable bridesmaid gowns at inexpensive rates, and these are an excellent option provided that they have an appropriate return policy.

If you are buying your bridesmaid gowns, make certain to pick something that they can utilize in the future, allowing them to get much more usage out of it.

How to Save Money

If you want a designer dress, think about working with a neighborhood seamstress to produce it for you. This could be a simple method to have the wedding event dress of your dreams without the large price tag connected. Just bring in a number of pictures of the dress you like, and go over choices with a competent seamstress.

When it pertains to your veil, you could enliven a low priced veil with a tulle tiara or budget-friendly jeweled to offer it a unique appearance, without spending a lot on a long beaded veil.

Chapter 4: Getting Deals on a Wedding Cake

The wedding cake is among the essential elements of the wedding reception. The cake is going to decorate the primary table, and visitors ought to admire its elegance. The cake is going to feature prominently in pictures of the reception, and it is going to be the primary attraction as the groom and bride cut it.

The cake should not just be aesthetically sensational, it ought to taste excellent as well. Lots of pastry shops focus a lot on making stunning wedding cakes that they appear to forget that the cake is going to be consumed! You ought to check out a variety of different pastry shops, not just to get quotes and take a look at samples, yet additionally to taste a few of their products. A lot of pastry shops are going to want to provide you with a taste testing in case you call in advance.

Make sure to select a cake which is going to interest both the groom and bride, not just in the look, yet additionally taste. The groom and bride ought to agree on the kind of cake they wish to have, however, the bride-to-be generally has the last word.

In many cases, there is a groom's cake as well. In case there will be both a bride-to-be's cake and a groom's cake, they can either select both together, or they could each select one individually. Keep in mind, however, the cake that is typically cut together is the bride-to-be's cake, and it ought to be fancier and bigger than the groom's cake.

Often you might have the ability to get a bargain on a cake by permitting the pastry shop to offer you the cake they pick. Numerous bakers like to get particularly imaginative, and they are, in some cases, ready to offer you a discount rate in case they can make a cake based upon their own vision. These kinds of cakes are great for their portfolio, and it is very special for them when they are offered unlimited freedom to develop whatever they desire.

Frequently, a cake that is merely embellished is going to be less expensive than a cake that needs lots of hours of work. Similarly, cakes which are iced in buttercream frosting have a tendency to be cheaper than cakes iced with fondant.

Straightforward cakes with a couple of fillings are going to be less labor-intensive and, for that reason, more affordable than cakes with unique fillings and flavors. Call local pastry shops in your location and get price quotes based upon all attendees you are having.

The majority of couples are choosing to have tinier, less complicated cakes nowadays. Certain couples are allowing their parents to bake straightforward cakes for the wedding event. It definitely spares cash, however, it could be dreadful in case the cakes don't turn out well. In case you are going to enable a relative to bake your cake, be sure they understand what they are doing!

A wedding cake could cost a few hundred dollars, so it is essential to attempt to spare cash when you are able to. Simply keep in mind that the cake is one part of the wedding event that is going to be captured on film, and you want for it to be a thing you are going to take pride in for the remainder of your lives.

How to Save Money

Frequently, supermarket bakeries are going to additionally make wedding cakes at a far more affordable price than neighborhood pastry shops.

Chapter 5: Saving Cash on Reception

Of all the expenses related to your wedding event, your reception could be among the greatest expenses of all, particularly if you are leasing space or utilizing in house caterers. Discuss what your perfect reception place would be, and after that, research possible areas in your location by calling the venues and inquiring about accessibility, prices and featured items.

When utilizing caterers which are supplied by the venue, you could anticipate paying 35% more than what you would pay if you used an outside catering service. Nevertheless, there are lots of places that demand that you utilize their in-house suppliers, so make certain to inquire about this when calling every place.

One terrific method to start your research is by utilizing the Web and searching through various locations in your area. Frequently, reception halls are going to publish details concerning catering services, pricing, and accessibility , and in case this information isn't offered, you can decide to get in touch with the management by e-mail before calling, to see if it is practical for your wedding based upon your assigned budget plan.

Produce a list of prospective reception areas focusing on the following:

Schedule And Accessibility: Are these places free for your big day?

Expense: Identify if the price is on a per-person basis or a flat fee (flat fees are generally less expensive based upon the number of attendees).

Inclusions and Decorations: Figure out whether decors, including table fabrics, candle lights, flowers, centerpieces, and other décor, are incorporated in the overall price.

Capacity: Ask how many attendees the location can accommodate, along with the different seating plans that might be offered. Particular places can hold more attendees depending upon whether they have long tables as opposed to round.

Constraints: Discover whether there are any particular constraints or requirements so as to reserve and utilize the hall. For instance, particular locations are not going to enable candle lights because of insurance coverage expenses and fire hazards, while others are not going to enable specific seating plans for identical reasons.

Catering: Figure out whether you have the ability to bring your own catering service to the place or if you have to utilize their on-site personnel. If so, figure out the total expenses for your reception. If you need to utilize their personnel or advised catering services, demand a complete list of available catering services and call every one separately.

Parking: Make certain that there is enough parking based upon all the attendees attending, along with guaranteeing that there is wheelchair access if needed.

Time Frame: You are going to wish to figure out how long the place is available, and more notably, whether there is another wedding event happening on an identical day. This could have a substantial influence on how good the reception goes, specifically, in case you are dealing with a time crunch or the location has to get ready for another reception after yours. If another wedding event is occurring on an identical day, make certain that it ends or starts 2 hours after yours to make certain that your partner, you, and your attendees have a lot of time to delight in your occasion.

If feasible, attempt to select a location that hosts just one wedding a day. When you have actually explored your alternatives and have a list of possible locations, it is time to connect with everyone directly. You could pick to do this yourself or entrust it to a member of the family or a friend.

Make a note of the list of questions which you have and make certain you go over everything prior to booking your reception at any location. The list ought to consist of:

1) How many members of the staff are assigned to your wedding event?

2) Does the location offer seating plans featuring chairs and tables, or do you have to lease them yourself?

3) Does the place have a bar, dance floor and where are the the band or DJ going to be located?

4) Does the place consist of a bridal room or location where you can change from your wedding event dress into your reception attire after supper?

5) Is there a minimum hour duration when it comes to your reception? Particular places are going to need a 4-5 hour minimum where you pay per hour.

No matter what place you pick, ensure that you drop by personally prior to booking it! A location could look substantially different face to face than in pictures, and you actually want to get a feel for the area, guaranteeing that it is roomy enough, along with whether it appears tidy and well kept.

Chapter 6: Saving Money on Reception Dinner

When you need to utilize an in house catering service, there is very little you are going to have the ability to do to spare cash besides picking less costly food products. A buffet has a tendency to be less expensive than a sit-down dinner, and soda just reception is less expensive than a reception with a complete bar.

Talk about your choices with the venue's catering service before working out your menu details. Numerous catering services have a variety of services, varying from cold and hot appetizers to the served or buffet dinners. Your selection of bars and some catering services is even going to involve the cake.

The food which is served can spare you cash also. More affordable meals like chicken or pasta could be just as nice, yet more economical than costly cuts of meat or costly seafood meals.

If you desire some of the seafood meals or costly meat, work with your catering service to see if they may do a seafood appetizer rather than it being the main dish. Your attendees are going to delight in mini-crab cakes instead of having them as a meal, and you are going to spare cash.

Having the ability to work with an outdoors catering service is going to provide you with a great deal of space to compare prices and services. Research catering services in your location; the reception location ought to have the ability to suggest catering services that other brides have actually utilized, or you could browse the web or specialized wedding sites.

Word of mouth is additionally a terrific resource-- speak to individuals you know who are newlywed, or who have actually gone to weddings just recently. Create a list of catering services which you have an interest in, and ask the this:

- Cost per Person-- get a grasp of their cost per head for a served dinner, a buffet dinner, with/without appetizers, excluding/including a complete bar, and so on. You wish to get an estimate for each circumstance to compare costs to other catering services. Lots of catering services are going to provide you with a hard copy price listing.

- Personnel-- discover how many staff is going to be participating in the wedding event. This is typically based upon whether your dinner is buffet or seated, and the number of attendees you have.

- Cake-- discover if the cake is featured with the catering services. If the cake is not featured, learn if your catering service is going to charge a fee to slice and offer the cake from the third-party.

- Bar-- learn if the catering service can offer a bar and alcohol (if wanted) and if they are going to be offering their personal bartender(s).

- Linens-- Will the catering service offer table linens? Is there an additional expense for linens for a present table?

- Centerpieces-- A catering service is often going to supply their own centerpieces at no additional charge

- Alternative meals-- as opposed to a seated dinner or a a buffet, are they happy to accommodate champagne brunch and a cake, or an appetizer only occasion?

When looking into your catering choices, don't forget to take into consideration if you are going to be offering alcohol.

When you have narrowed down your selection of catering services, establish the time with every one of them in order to try out their food. Bring your fiancé or another individual near to you to tasting, and take notes as you are there. Select the catering service that ideally fits your budget plan and requirements.

Chapter 7: Catering

Catering is definitely a fundamental portion of the wedding party. You are going to wish to work carefully with the catering service to pick a menu that is going to work for both the groom and bride.

You are going to additionally want to be aware of the tastes of any prospective attendees. Generally, there would be a number of various main dishes to select from, however, nowadays, you need to have other dietary needs in mind as well. Although you can't be expected to offer every dietary requirement, you might want to offer vegetarian options if you understand there are going to be vegetarians there.

Preferably you would need to know well ahead of time if anybody participating has unique dietary needs. If feasible, ask attendees to notify you of their requirements when they RSVP.

Talk about these requirements with the catering service well ahead of time so they can make plans.

Often, they are going to want to make unique accommodations, so they want to learn about this ahead of time to set all the things up appropriately.

Individuals that have unique dietary requirements are generally accustomed to bringing their own food to occasions, so don't panic if a vegetarian appears unannounced. It's not the end of the world! However, being ready does assist if this occurs. It's constantly an excellent idea to advise your catering service to at least offer one vegan appetizer so that potential vegetarians could have a thing to nibble on.

When picking appetizers, it is ideal to choose finger foods which aren't really messy. Attendees are going to be wearing really pricey clothes most likely, and you don't want them to have any unneeded cleaning expenses! Foods such as shrimp cocktail and barbecue are probably off the menu. Cleaner foods such as finger sandwiches and pâté are great options.

The main dish could usually be messier, however, make sure to have at least 2 courses to pick from.

Your fiancée and you might delight in steak, for instance, however, you ought to have a fish or chicken option for those who don't consume red meat.

Weddings ought to be centered around the groom and bride, however, the other attendees ought to be made to feel as pleased as feasible. The happier the attendees are, the more wonderful the day is going to be for everybody, and that is going to all be recorded!

Chapter 8: Sparing Cash On Flowers

Flowers could be an extremely costly part of a wedding event. Lots of people spend hundreds, even 1000s of dollars on the flowers for their wedding event. However, there are some techniques you could utilize to make certain you get lovely flowers without spending excessive cash.

Firstly, don't pick roses or other costly flowers unless you are truly sure you desire them. Lots of brides pick roses just due to the fact they think it is standard or the norm. However, nowadays, nearly any kind of flower is appropriate for a wedding event. You can constantly decide to include more affordable flowers like carnations into a bouquet with a couple of more costly types. Or, you might pick one gorgeous flower as an alternative to a whole bouquet.

Take care when it comes to color options. Certain flower colors are more uncommon than others, and those colors are going to be more costly. Go over the costs of various colors with your floral designer, and pick one that is budget-friendly, but also the one that is going to make you pleased.

You do want to synchronize the colors of the flowers with other colors, so that is also a thing to consider. However, the flowers don't need to match the color of the bridesmaid gowns or other aspects, provided that they don't clash.

You might have the ability to utilize fewer flowers than necessary. Certain brides go for it and select flower plans for each single reception table, and they even have a bouquet for each bridesmaid. However, this isn't required.

You could speak to your fiancé regarding the arrangement of flowers, along with the floral designer and the maid of honor. Talk to figure out which arrangements are essential, and which may be excluded to save money.

The most crucial thing to bear in mind is to make certain you get the flowers you actually desire. Your big day is possibly the most remarkable day of your whole life, and ideally, you are just going to have one. It ought to be a day you are going to keep in mind permanently, and eventually, you want to be certain you are receiving what makes you most happy.

In case you are supplying your own centerpieces for your tables, you have numerous choices. You could develop flower centerpieces out of silk or fresh flowers in case you are developing the flowers for the remainder of your wedding event. In case you don't want flowers, you could float petals in water bowls or fill glass bowls with colored beads for a beautiful appearance that won't set you back too much.

Candlelight arrangements additionally make beautiful centerpieces and could be affordable in case you purchase candle lights in bulk, or with vouchers.

In case you are not utilizing a floral designer, you could organize the flowers personally. It might be simpler to utilize silk flowers in this scenario since they could be set up far ahead of time, and they might be bought at a discount rate or by utilizing vouchers.

In case you do decide to deal with a floral designer, talk with them about the ideal flowers to utilize for the season of your wedding event. Flowers in season are going to be more affordable and they are going to hold up much better.

How to Save Money

When employing a floral designer, never ever point out the reality that the flowers are for your wedding event up until the price has actually been worked out! The word "wedding" is frequently going to induce a hijack in price, so remember that when thinking about using professional floral designers.

Chapter 9: How to Save Cash on Invites

When it pertains to prepping and sending your invites, you are going to wish to attempt to send them within 6 and 10 weeks before your wedding event with an RSVP date of at least 2 weeks before (ideally 3-4 to ensure that you can get ready).

This permits your attendees to reply and let you understand whether they can make it or not, and offers you the time to identify how many attendees are very likely to show up at, in case you have to follow up with your reception supplier.

Begin by producing a "prospective" attendee list, and after that, if needed, weed through the list and figure out simply how many people you can manage to invite. In case you are having a sit-down supper, you are going to want to pay for every plate, so remember this when making the guest list.

Don't feel forced to invite everybody you know. This is your day, and you ought to invite just those who mean the most to you, specifically when working within a limited budget plan.

As soon as you have your guest list figured out, you are going to want to buy invites in addition to envelope and stamps inserts to ensure that those getting your invites can answer, letting you know whether they have the ability to show up or not.

When it pertains to buying your invites, they are going to vary in cost from really budget-friendly for standard invitation plans, to exceptionally costly ones if you have an interest in pricey, tailored invites.

In case you have a bigger guest list, think about selecting a straightforward yet classy style that is going to cost less per bundle and might feature return envelopes too.

If you truly wish to spare cash, you might make your own invites by utilizing your personal computer and paper stock with a printer. You could download beautiful invite design templates from sites for little or no charge, or if you are the imaginative type, you might even create your own invites utilizing scrapbook components, even though this might take a while if your attendee list is a prolonged one.

Contact your local stationery shop for budget-friendly card stock, and in case you are printing your own invites in your home, utilize a top quality laser printer for finest outcomes.

How to Save Money

Instead of including a return envelope with a stamp, think about including your e-mail address or phone number to minimize postage expenses.

Chapter 10: How to Save Cash on Wedding Music

Based upon the kind of wedding event you are hosting, you might wish to have music played throughout your wedding in addition to dance and reception. Picking a DJ is constantly a much more budget-friendly choice than employing a band unless you know somebody who is knowledgeable and happy to do this.

In case you are having your ceremony in a temple or church, consult them to see if music is going to be supplied and what the cost is for the offered music. Certain couples want to have outside music playing, for instance, violinist or a cantor, at their own cost.

Employing a musician from the outside to play music for your ceremony might cost a great deal of cash. If you wish to have something precious played at your event, yet you wish to spare cash, check in with your family and friends to see if anybody is a skilled entertainer and would have the ability to supply their services to you.

If your event is not in a temple or church, yet at the identical area as your reception, you might have the option of DJ or a band playing music for both your reception and ceremony.

A DJ is going to bring his/her own music and tools, or you can offer music to them to play. A band can differ from a couple of individuals to a full stage, based upon the kind of band.

Generally, a DJ is less costly than a band since you are just paying someone. If you do not want live music, a DJ is a terrific alternative due to the fact that they are going to offer MC services together with any music you want.

When calling your musicians, inquire about the following:

- Do you charge a per hour rate or a flat rate?

- How early prior to the reception/ceremony are you going to show up to establish your devices?

- Do I have to supply any music?

- Do you have the capability to play special tracks which we want to have?

- Throughout the reception, are you going to take requests or are you going to have a set list?

- May we offer you a list of tracks that we do not want to hear?

When you have actually chosen the band or DJ that you want to utilize, keep the agreement with all of your wedding documentation.

Chapter 11: Photography And Videography Money Savers

The videos and photos of your wedding are going to be mementos which you are going to treasure permanently.

Your media quality, either photos or video, is based upon the individual taking the video or pictures in addition to the quality of their devices. Videographers and photographers could be extremely costly, even for the most affordable bundles they offer.

Certain photographers are going to offer video service, yet generally, if you want to have both video and pictures, you are going to need to work with 2 different individuals.

If you wish to have professional photos, you might have a buddy or member of the family recording a video of your wedding event. Some couples additionally decide not to have their wedding event taped on video. Consider your choices and what is going to be best for your budget plan and desires.

Research professional photographers thoroughly as you would anything else in your wedding event. Search the phone book and web, and ask your family and friends. Your suppliers might additionally have the ability to suggest a great photographer.

When you are getting in touch with a professional photographer, ask what video camera they utilize for taking pictures. Certain professional photographers are just going to utilize digital, some are just going to utilize film, and after that, others are going to utilize a mix. Additionally, discover if they have an assistant which is going to be with them.

Photographers frequently provide package deals. These typically consist of some mix of printed photos, digital photos, and CDs (if the photographer is utilizing a digital camera), picture albums, and hours of service.

Contact a number of professional photographers and get quotes, and after that, meet a couple of them to see their portfolios. Select a professional photographer with a style comparable to yours. Perhaps you would like a creative kind of album.

A great method to spare cash with a qualified photographer is to discover somebody who utilizes digital and buy their most affordable bundle which consists of all of the digital pictures on a CD.

In case you have all of the photos on CD without copyright, you are going to have the ability to print them at a printer, on the web, or utilizing your personal computer, and just purchase what you require. Additionally, know the number of hours you are going to require a professional photographer for.

In case you desire expert pictures of getting dressed in your dress, you might need to pay more for their additional travel and time.

You might conserve cash in case you have a buddy or member of the family taking pictures during the day while utilizing the expert photographer just for the reception and event.

The identical suggestions go for a videographer-- research your options properly, select somebody with a design comparable to your own, and select the least pricey bundle which is going to supply you with what you require.

In case you are seeking to spare as much cash as feasible, you could look into other sources to discover a professional photographer and/or videographer.

Brand-new businesses which are start-ups are going to frequently video or photo your wedding event at a really affordable price since they are going to have the ability to utilize your video/photos for a portfolio.

You could additionally attempt to find trainees at colleges, art schools and nearby community colleges with an interest in videography or photography. They are going to want to work at more affordable pay since they are aiming to get experience and excellent recommendations.

Chapter 11: Honeymoon

It appears that the only locations individuals consider when you talk about "honeymoon" are Hawaii and Niagara Falls! However, there are numerous gorgeous and unique areas that could be just as romantic. In case you are not a Niagara Falls fan, don't fret!

In case the two of you are huge outdoor fan, why not organize a camping honeymoon? A peaceful mountain cabin close to a babbling brook and evening hours by a roaring campfire could be equally as romantic as any beach! And in case the two of you enjoy beaches, bear in mind that Hawaii isn't the only lovely area for a romantic honeymoon. There are numerous beautiful beaches in America alone, and a lot of them are a lot quieter and a lot more charming than Hawaii!

If you like crowds, Hawaii may be a terrific option, however numerous couples like a bit more intimacy and privacy. Search for isolated beaches which provide more privacy if you believe the two of you would enjoy more time alone.

Europe is a prominent location for lots of couples. There are a lot of romantic tours of a few of Europe's most romantic cities. You might devote a week enjoying the sights of Paris, Venice, Rome, London, and Madrid.

A cruise is another excellent idea. If you two are huge fans of the ocean, a cruise may be simply what you are trying to find! And don't anticipate spending all of your time on a boat! Lots of cruises have numerous landfall destinations where you are able to go ashore and hang out shopping and taking in the sights.

The honeymoon is a thing the two of you ought to both delight in. If you like the beach, yet your fiancé can't stand it, a tropical trip may not be the ideal option. You may be dissatisfied due to the fact that you didn't get your dream honeymoon in Barbados, however, you two are going to have a far more unforgettable honeymoon supposing that you compromise and pick a mutually satisfying place together!

Conclusion

Your wedding event is among the most special days of your life, and both your partner and you ought to have the ability to honor your love without the tension due to debt from getting loans to pay for your big day.

It' s crucial to think beyond the big day, and to start your married life in a manner that allows you both to carry on enjoying one another, instead of struggling for several years to settle a loan.

Set your budget plan and utilize ideas and techniques within this book to guarantee that you remain within this price range when planning your wedding event. You could have a lovely wedding event without spending a great deal while doing so, if you take your time, remain arranged and on track.

I hope that you enjoyed reading through this book and that you have found it useful. If you want to share your thoughts on this book, you can do so by leaving a review on the Amazon page. Have a great rest of the day.

Printed in Great Britain
by Amazon

24954205R00040